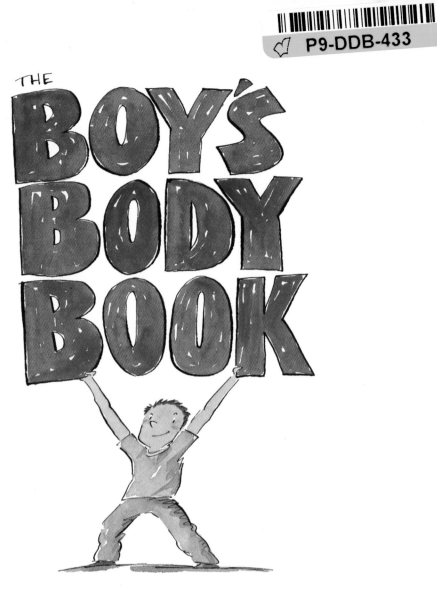

THE BOY'S BODY BOOK

Written by Kelli Dunham

Illustrated by Steve Bjorkman

CIDER MILL PRESS

BOOK PUBLISHERS

Kennebunkport, Maine

Applesauce Press is an imprint of
Cider Mill Press Book Publishers

13 Digit ISBN: 978-1-933662-74-9
10 Digit ISBN: 1-933662-74-3

This book may be ordered by mail from the publisher.
Please include $2.50 for postage and handling.
Please support your local bookseller first!

Books published by Cider Mill Press Book Publishers are available at special discounts for bulk purchases in the United States by corporations, institutions, and other organizations.
For more information, please contact the publisher.

Library of Congress Control Number: 2007921663

Applesauce Press is an imprint of
Cider Mill Press Book Publishers
"Where good books are ready for press"
12 Port Farm Road
Kennebunkport, Maine 04046

Visit us on the web!
www.cidermillpress.com

Design by Alicia Freile
Typography: Block, Century Schoolbook, Frutiger, and Rockwell
Printed in China

Special thanks and acknowledgment to Josalyn Moran, an inspiration to every children's book publisher... and especially to us!

Dedicated to Heather Ann MacAllister, who every day makes the world a happier and safer place to be a growing boy.

-K.D.

Table of Contents

What on Earth is Going On Around Here? Your Changing Body 38

Your Changing Body in the Outside World 54

4

Changes at Home 76

5

Your Changing Feelings and Friends 88

Resources and Further Reading 102

What's Changing?

AT THIS TIME in your life, on some days it might seem like… everything!

Your **body** is changing.

Your **feelings** are changing.

Your **relationships** with your friends and family members are changing.

It hardly seems fair, does it?

Especially because often as a boy gets older, he finds that it gets more difficult to talk with the adults in his life about the kind of things he used to. There are a few very good reasons for this:

He might be afraid to ask a question he thinks he should already know the answer to.

He might feel like he doesn't know the best (or the most polite) word to use to describe something that is happening with his body.

He might be worried that something he is feeling isn't normal, and that people would laugh at him if they knew what was going on in his head (or his body!).

Not very fun, but it is 100 percent normal!

And it isn't just kids who sometimes develop troubles communicating. You may

have noticed that sometimes the adults around you have trouble talking about the changes you are going through.

It seems like they should be able to handle it, since they've been through this hard "kid to adult" transition themselves. So what are they worried about? Mostly the same things you are!

They might worry about not having all the right information.

They might remember how awkward this time was for them and feel like they don't have any advice to help you get through it.

They might even be worried (does this sound familiar?) of not knowing the correct or polite terms for body parts and body processes.

And especially, they might be worried about giving you more information than you want to know or are ready for.

So with boys and adults all red-faced and stammering and stuttering it makes it hard for information to flow back and forth. That's where this book comes in.

This book has a lot of information about the changes that are coming your way. We hope it will answer many of your questions so that you feel more ready and informed and less confused and scared.

There is no right or wrong way to use this book. You are the expert on how to make it work best for you!

You might want to sit right down and read it from cover to cover, all at once (maybe under the covers with a flashlight, if you are feeling particularly shy).

You might just look at the chapters that interest you for now, and then put it on your shelf until you have more questions about the other stuff in the rest of the book.

If you aren't interested or don't want to know about the stuff in this book, no problem. You can always put the book away until later when you want to know more!

This is just one small book so it can't contain the answers for every question that you might have about this exciting—but sometimes confusing—time of your life. Again, a trusted adult comes in handy here. If something written here doesn't make sense

to you, or is different from your experience, discuss it with a parent, teacher, health care provider, or another responsible, trusted grown-up.

Although this time is not easy, you already have many resources for dealing with the changes that are coming your way. You have past experiences that you have learned from. You have friends that are going through the same things you are, and you have adults who care about you. All these things will help make the process smoother. Best of luck to you as you begin the important transition of growing from a boy into a man.

Quick Tip

If you don't like to read, (there are probably lots of guys who wish someone would develop an "all about your changing body" video game) you can ask an adult you trust to read through this book with you. Maybe you can use it as a starting point for a discussion about any questions you have.

CHAPTER 1

The Care And Feeding Of Your Changing Body

Hygiene (Hey, What's That SMELL?)

It seems like it could be nature's joke that just when boys' sweat glands begin to work overtime, boys often develop what looks like an allergy to bathing. If you are struggling with the adults in your life about taking a bath (which does cut into video game playing time), remember this: Now that you are growing up, you have more adult-like sweat glands. This means you are going to have more of an adult-like smell. Even though you may not be able to tell the difference, people around you will. Especially at school, if you get the reputation as the "stinky kid," it could be very hard to lose.

Hit The Showers

Showering (or taking a bath) every day (or at least every other day) is your first line of defense when it comes to the "smellies." For best results, wash all your parts (from your head to your feet). Remember to use soap. Soap is an important part of this process and sometimes boys forget. If you have noticed that you are particularly smelly, you can get special soap labeled "deodorant," which will help keep you odor-free longer. It's best not to use deodorant soap all over your body though, because it can really dry out your skin. Just use it for your smelliest parts (usually your armpits and your feet).

Quick Tip

Taking a shower before you go to bed at night will help you get out the door faster in the morning. However, if you are particularly worried about the smellies, or you and your brother like to wrestle at night after you take your shower, a morning bath or shower is probably the way to go.

Get Dressed

Showering every day helps, but you also need to change your clothes as regularly as you can to keep you smelling good. Unfortunately, you can't tell by looking at it if a piece of clothing is clean or dirty. For example, a tee-shirt that you wore to school all day might not have an obvious spot or stain on it, but if you sniff the underarms? *Pee-ooo.* That's why it's best to keep your dirty clothes and your clean clothes far away from each other. That way you will be able to know the difference without doing the "sniff" test, which might not tell you for sure anyway.

Lotion: It's Not Just For Girls

You, yes you, can use lotion. Some boys will need lotion after a shower to keep from having dry, flaky, itchy skin. You can get lotion made especially for boys, and you can also get lotion that doesn't have any smell added to it at all. If you put in on while you are still damp from the shower, it will be a smoother process. You might even find that you like how it feels.

Deodorant Works

Another possible weapon in your personal fight against "the smellies" is deodorant. Not everyone (even grown-ups) wears or needs deodorant, but if you want to try it, look for the type that says only "deodorant" and not "deodorant/anti-perspirant." Anti-perspirant contains chemicals which actually block your sweat glands, which is not as healthy for your body. Some deodorants have a stronger smell than others, so you might have to try a few different kinds to find what smells best on you.

Wash Those Hands

Hand washing is another important personal hygiene issue to talk about, and the good thing is that you don't even have to get completely wet to do it! Hand washing is not just about *personal* hygiene, because germs on your hands (which you use to touch everything) can make you (and people around you) sick. Sometimes it seems to boys that grown-ups are too worried about hand washing, but it is pretty important. If you eat without washing your hands, it's like (and yes, this is gross) putting everything that you've touched since the last time you washed your hands… right in your mouth.

Not a very nice thought, is it? Yuck!

It's also very important to wash your hands after you use the toilet, after petting or handling any kind of animal, and if you have been around someone who is sick.

You already know how to wash your hands, right? Well, maybe so, but most people don't wash their hands long enough. It really takes 15 to 20 seconds under warm water (with soap) to get them clean. You might want to use a timer (or just count slowly to yourself) to make sure you're washing long enough. Sometimes dirt can get trapped under your nails: there are soft bristled brushes that can help with that.

Heading Out: Hair

Boys have it pretty easy when it comes to what people expect them to do with their hair. Regular shampooing (which might mean every day if you have oily hair or are very active) should just about do it.

Some boys use gel to make their hair stay in place. Some gels wash out easily, but some (especially ones that are

KNOW THE FACTS

Germs cannot be seen by your eyes so you have no way of knowing if they are on your hands. The warmth of your body combined with sweat allows germs to grow quickly.

wax-based) are much harder to get out. If you are going to use a wax-based gel or hair-molding product, you'll have to wash it out every night if you don't want to wake up in the morning with your hair looking like something from a horror movie.

If you have longer or particularly tangly hair, you can buy conditioner which you can use after you shampoo. You can also buy special shampoos for very dry hair (to keep you from having dandruff, which is when skin from your scalp flakes off and makes a mess) and shampoos for hair that is exposed a lot to chlorine (for boys on a swim team).

The Ear From Which You Hear

The most important thing to remember about ears is: don't stick anything smaller than your elbow in them. That means no cotton tip swabs, no pen caps, and no paper clips! All these items

can really hurt your ears if you stick them too deep. If you are shampooing your hair regularly, that should be enough to keep your ears clean. Still, it doesn't hurt to spend a little extra time with a washcloth, scrubbing behind your ears. If you have short hair, the dirt that builds up in that area can be very noticeable!

The wax you have in your ears is helpful: it keeps dirt from getting further down into your ear where it can do real damage. Although it might be tempting to pick at it, it's better to leave the wax alone and let it do its job. If your ears feel clogged or you have trouble hearing, talk with your health care provider about things you can do to help get rid of some of the wax.

The Expert Says

Have you seen how little kids hold their hands over their ears when something making a loud sound (like a fire engine with the siren blaring) goes by? They are smart because they know that loud sounds can hurt their ears. The headphones you wear when you play your I-pod or stereo can also hurt your ears if it is too loud. Chances are that if other people can hear your music when you are wearing headphones it is too loud. When you are old, you'll be thankful that you turned down the volume!

What's That Spot: The Ins And Outs, Ups And Downs Of Acne

It might seem like some kind of mysterious plague, but there are some things you can do to tame the "zit monster."

● Washing your face can help reduce acne, but don't do it too often. If you wash your face more than three times a day or too harshly (you can't scrub your face like you scrub a dirty pan!) washing will irritate acne, not make it better.

● Don't pick! It can irritate your skin and cause an infection, and maybe even a permanent scar.

● You can buy creams at the drugstore to help with acne. Follow the directions and don't use more than the label says because benzoyl peroxide (the most common ingredient in over-the-counter acne creams) can be very irritating if you use too much.

● If you feel like your acne is out of control, talk with the adults in your life about going to a dermatologist, a doctor that specializes in skin.

Putting Your Best Face Forward

The easiest way to take care of the skin on your face is to keep it clean. You can wash your face when you wash your hands, but try to use a gentle, non-perfumed soap. Don't use deodorant soap because it will leave a light film of deodorant on your face, and no one (no matter how smelly) needs deodorant on their face.

Another very common problem that boys have with the skin on their face is acne.

Who gets acne? Almost everyone! Nine out of ten pre-teens and teenagers have to deal with it. Acne is caused when excess oil becomes trapped in your pores, combines with bacteria (i.e. germs) and dead skin cells and develops what we call a pimple.

Shaving

The first place you will probably have hair on your face is on your upper lip and chin. It will probably be just a little teeny amount (like the fuzz on a peach). You can remove this by shaving or by using a special depilatory powder made for men and boys who get "bumps" when they shave.

There is no medical reason to remove the hair from your face, but many boys find they are more comfortable without it. If you do decide to shave, when you first start you might only need to do it every few days because the hair won't grow that quickly.

The best way to learn about shaving is to talk to a male adult in your life (or an older brother) and get him to show you how to do it. For many boys, their first shave feels like an important part of becoming an adult.

Quick Tip

Shave with the grain! This means you should shave in the direction of how the hair grows on your face. Shaving against the grain can cause redness, rashes, razor burn and ingrown hairs, which can be painful.

Keeping Your Awesome Smile Looking Awesome

As you get older, the adults in your life will start expecting you to take more responsibility for things, including your oral hygiene (which is a fancy way of saying mouth care). And even though there is no longer an adult standing over you making sure you brush your teeth, now is the time build good habits that will keep your teeth looking good for a lifetime.

You probably know someone (maybe a grandparent) who has lost their teeth and now has fake ones that they take out at night and keep in a cup by the bed! We know a lot more about dental care now than we did when they were young, so losing your teeth to tooth decay does not have to be a usual part of getting older.

A good smile = A great first impression

Let's Brush!

The foundation of all oral care is brushing your teeth. You probably think you're an expert, but for a quick review:

Step #1: Pick the right brush. A brush with bristles labeled "medium" or "hard" will be too tough on your gums and can actually contribute to gum disease! A toothbrush with worn out bristles won't get your teeth squeaky clean, so it works best if you replace your toothbrush every three to four months.

#2. Use toothpaste that contains fluoride, which, as you probably have heard on toothpaste commercials, is the ingredient that fights cavities.

#3. To start, brush the outside surfaces of your teeth (another way of saying this is the side that touches the inside of your cheek). Move the toothbrush back and forth, but in small strokes, and do a few teeth at a time. You will have to do it several times in each spot.

#4. When you are done brushing the outside of your teeth, brush the inside.

#5. Also brush the flat surfaces of your teeth (the chewing surface)

#6. Finally, brush your tongue. Your tongue can hold on to bacteria that can make your breath super-smelly!

#7. In order to really clean your teeth, you need to brush them for 2-3 minutes. Use a stop watch or the timer on the microwave to make sure you are brushing long enough.

#8. Don't forget to floss!

Brushing is the most important thing you can do to keep your pearly whites, uh, pearly white. Besides brushing, flossing is another important thing you can do to help your teeth and gums stay healthy. Flossing removes food bits and bacteria from between your teeth. It helps avoid cavities and keeps your gums strong.

Do I Have To Go?
Boys And The Dentist

Although you can do a lot to help your teeth and mouth stay healthy at home, you also need a check-up and cleaning at the dentist's office every six months. Not all families have health insurance, and not all health insurance plans cover going to the dentist, but there are still ways to get dental care. Your school nurse can probably give you some ideas of how the adults in your life can make that happen.

Some people (not just kids) don't like going to the dentist. If this is the case for you, make sure you ask questions before you get to the dentist's office. Ask the adult who made the appointment for you why you have the appointment: are you only having your teeth cleaned or do you need something more done? Then, when you get to the dentist's office, before you open your mouth and say "ahhh," ask the dental hygienist or the dentist to explain exactly what is going to happen, step by step. Some procedures at the dentist's office might be uncomfortable, and the more information you have about when and how things might not feel so good, the more you can prepare yourself. A surprise birthday party might be a fun thing, but not a surprise in the dentist's chair!

Tiny Little Train Tracks: The Drama Of Braces

Lots of kids (and adults even) have braces. But even though braces are very common, sometimes even hearing that they MIGHT have to get braces makes boys sweat.

The most common reasons people need braces are because their teeth are crooked or because their upper and lower jaws are not the same size. Both of these problems can make it harder to care for your teeth. Braces don't just improve your smile: they can make your entire mouth healthier.

Getting braces is a perfect

The Expert Says

Some foods are off-limits when you have braces. Ask your orthodontist before eating anything particularly sticky, such as caramels or gummy candy.

time to start taking more responsibility for your health. Ask your orthodontist about how you should care for your braces, what kind of foods you should avoid, and what you should do if part of your braces breaks off, gets bent, or irritates the inside of your mouth.

Meet Your Feet

Feet can be some of the **smelliest** parts of the body. This is because nearly everyone's feet sweat a lot. And since bacteria that can contribute to smelliness grow best in places that are not only damp, but also dark, you can see why taking off your shoes after a long hot day can sometimes be a frightening experience!

Foot care is really no

Avoid Those Athlete's Feet

Athlete's foot is easy to catch if you walk around barefoot where many other people walk around barefoot (like a school locker room, for example, which is probably where the nickname came from). The best way to avoid getting it is to buy special flip flops that you wear only in the locker room or public shower and to wash and dry your feet well every day.

different than caring for any other part of your body, except that you have to wash your feet with a little more energy if you really want to get them clean. Make sure you separate each toe, because bacteria can get stuck in there and contribute to

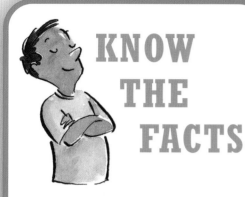

KNOW THE FACTS

Athlete's foot is caused by a fungus. Up to 70 percent of the population will get it at some time in their lives.

general smelliness. Make sure you dry your feet after and change your socks every day.

One common foot problem is called "athlete's foot," which is not caused by being an athlete. Athlete's foot is a fungus, and it can turn your feet into an itchy, smelly mess. If you have itchy feet and what looks like extra dry skin on the bottom of one or both of your feet (especially where your toes meet the ball of your foot) you might have athlete's foot. When you first get it, it can usually be treated with a special kind of medicine called an antifungal that the adult who is responsible for you can buy at almost any drugstore. It's important to treat athlete's foot right away because it can spread to even less fun parts of your body. Maybe you've heard of "jock itch?" Ewwww.

If the antifungal doesn't get rid of your athlete's foot, or if it spreads to the area on or near your toenails, you may need medicine you get from a health care provider to heal it up.

The Expert Says

Don't use anti-fungal medication in your genital area.

Fighting Temptation: Thinking About Drinking, Smoking, And Drugs

Hopefully, you are looking at this and thinking, "Why are they talking about this? I am way too young to even think about stuff like that." But unfortunately that's not true for all boys. In fact, 6 percent of all kids your age say they drink alcohol on a regular basis.

Even if you don't see many people in your life smoking, drinking alcohol, or using illegal drugs, you are still exposed to advertising for alcohol and tobacco products. And you have probably seen movies and TV shows that show people using illegal drugs. So you probably know some things about alcohol and drugs, even if they haven't touched your life directly.

The best place to get information about smoking, drugs, and alcohol is from an adult you trust. They especially need to know if someone asks you to try these things. It's important—but not always easy—to say "no" to drugs.

It's especially hard if there are lots of drugs around you. If this is true for you, talk with the adults that are

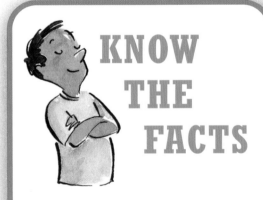

KNOW THE FACTS

Using marijuana can cause memory loss and learning problems. It can also affect your coordination.

Quick Tip

For more advice on saying no to drugs go to www.dea.gov/pubs/straight/cover.htm.

responsible for taking care of you about changing things in your environment (like where you live, where you go to school and what adults you are around) to help you stay drug-free. Even if you can't move or change schools, they can help you think up ways to make your environment safer; for example changing how you walk to school or finding different activities to be involved in after school.

One of the ways boys are pressured to use drugs is by someone presenting drinking, smoking or getting high as an adult thing to do. But facing your problems head on, and being "in the moment" (instead of being tuned out by illegal substances) is the best way to show how grown up you are.

The Expert Says

Lots of boys at this age like to try things that adults consider to be "risky" behavior. If you are looking to gain more independence, keep in mind that there are safe, constructive ways to do it. Don't feel like drugs or alcohol are the best way to "test your limits."

Other Things You Should Know About Smoking, Drugs, And Alcohol:

Illegal drugs are against the law for everyone. You can be arrested for having just a little in your pocket or in your backpack, you don't even have to be using it. But for kids, cigarettes and alcohol are also against the law. In the United States, it's illegal for kids under 18 to buy cigarettes and for anyone under 21 to buy alcohol.

Advertising for both alcohol and cigarettes makes these substances look fun and grown-up. But they don't show the aftereffects of smoking and drinking. For example, the commercial that shows people drinking with their friends, might not show one of the friends getting arrested for driving drunk. And the billboard that shows the big, manly cowboy smoking doesn't show him a few years later dying of lung cancer.

Even if you can't think about the bad things that could happen to you in the future if you use drugs or alcohol, here are some things that could happen right away: some drugs can hurt your brain and heart. Smoking is expensive and makes your breath, hair, and clothes stink. And alcohol and drugs may help you forget your problems for a little while, but they make it harder to think things through and make good decisions.

The Expert Says

Everyone wants to look good, but using steroids isn't the way to get there. All kinds of horrible things can happen to your body when you use steroids. Your testicles can shrink, you can grow breasts, you can lose your hair, get depressed, stop growing, or even die. Some of the effects of steroids are reversible. Some are not. Remember that a good body and better physical fitness is something you have to earn through practice and training, not through drugs. Don't risk your future just to have bulging biceps now!

Yawn! Boys And Sleep

When you were younger, your parents were more likely to enforce a strict bedtime. Now that you are older, you may still have a bedtime, but getting enough sleep is starting to become more and more your responsibility.

The average boy your age needs 10 hours of sleep a night in order to grow and be healthy. But you might need a little bit more or less than that. If you have trouble waking up in the morning, can't concentrate at school, or fall asleep during class, it might not be because you're bored. You just might not be getting enough sleep.

What if you have trouble getting to sleep? One of the things you can do to help yourself is to create a bedtime routine. If you do the same things every night, it will help your body recognize, "hey, it's time for sleeping now!"

Wetting The Bed

Some boys (many more than you might think) have trouble with wetting the bed, even into their teen years. It is so common, in fact, that this problem has a special name: nocturnal (nighttime) enuresis. Most often this is caused by being a very deep sleeper, but other things can contribute to it. Many times nocturnal enuresis runs in families, so if you wet the bed, there is a good chance that someone you see at the family reunion did too. If you are wetting the bed, talk to an adult in your life about it.

Quick Tip

If you tend to wake up in the middle of the night remembering, "Oh, I can't believe I didn't tell Mrs. Walker I can't mow her lawn next week," keep a pen and paper by your bed so you can jot these things down.

There are many simple things that can help with bedwetting, but it's best to get checked out by a doctor before you start any program of your own. This will make mornings (and sleepovers) a much more pleasant experience!

Some Other Tips For Getting A Good Night's Sleep

DO stay away from caffeine in the hours before you go to bed. You probably already know that certain types of soda contain caffeine, but did you know that chocolate does too?

DO avoid stimulating activities. For some boys this might mean not watching action or horror movies, reading exciting books, or playing "just until I reach the next level" of a video game, at least not right before bed. All these things are fun, but they aren't really relaxing.

DO avoid arguments or other things that might upset you emotionally right before you go to bed.

DO pack your bag and lay out your clothes for the next day. If you think you might forget something (like materials you need for a special project) write yourself a reminder note.

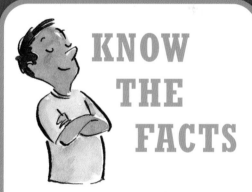

KNOW THE FACTS

Wetting the bed doesn't mean you are lazy or a slob. It's something you can't help doing. The good news is that most kids who wet the bed eventually stop.

CHAPTER 2

What On Earth Is Going On Around Here? Your Changing Body

IF YOU ARE a boy between the ages of 8 and 12, you have probably noticed some changes in your body. These changes are called *puberty*. Puberty is the general name for the process everyone goes through to change from a kid to an adult. Some of the changes are physical and some of the changes are emotional.

Puberty takes place over several years, and while it may seem like the process will never end, most boys are through puberty by age 16 or 17 or so.

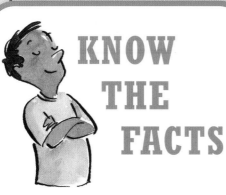

KNOW THE FACTS

Hormones are chemical messengers that help your cells communicate with each other. Everyone has hormones. In boys the hormone that controls puberty is called testosterone. In girls, it's called estrogen.

The changes your body will go through can seem a bit mysterious, but they basically result from one thing: extra amounts of special chemicals (called hormones) that start to be produced in your body. In boys, the hormone most responsible for puberty is called testosterone. You'll be hearing a lot more about testosterone in the pages ahead.

There's Something Going On Down There: Genital Changes

One of the first changes many boys notice when they start puberty is that their testicles (the glands that produce sperm and testosterone) start to get bigger, and the skin on their scrotum (the pouch of skin behind the penis that holds the testicles) gets darker. If this is happening to you, you may also have noticed that the skin on your scrotum is starting to look rougher too.

Another thing you may discover is that because you have more testosterone in your system, you may have more frequent erections. Males are able to have erections (when the penis gets hard and sticks out more) even as babies; this is normal. But when these erections start happening more often (especially for what seems like no reason at all!) it can feel pretty embarrassing. Most of the time, if you don't make a big deal out of it, no one will even notice you are having an erection. Especially if you are

Quick Tip

If you are worried that the people around you will notice when you have an erection, carry around an extra sweatshirt that you can keep on your lap.

around other kids your age, chances are they are too busy feeling self conscious about their own bodies to notice what is going on with yours!

The male reproductive system is a pretty amazing bit of plumbing. It consists of the penis, the scrotum, the testicles, and the urethra. As you go through puberty you'll notice that you grow pubic hair (hair around and above your penis) and that your penis gets larger.

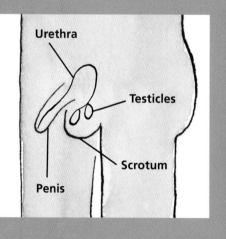

Urethra

Testicles

Scrotum

Penis

Morning Surprises

Another thing that can sometimes embarrasses boys going through puberty is something doctors call a "nocturnal emission" and everyone else calls a "wet dream." A wet dream is when some semen (the sticky liquid that is stored in the testicles) comes out from a boy's penis while he is asleep. Sometimes when this happens a boy remembers a certain type of dream; other times he just notices a wet spot on his pajamas or on the sheets after he wakes up.

If you don't know about this in advance, a wet dream can seem weird or even a little scary. But wet dreams are a normal part of development. They will stop happening as you get older.

Quick Tip

Some boys get embarrassed when they have a wet dream because the semen can make a mark on the sheets. If you feel this way, you might want to negotiate with your parents to do your own laundry. Then you'll be happy because you will be the only one who knows when you have a wet dream. Your parents will also be happy since it means they will have less laundry to do!

Who Is That Person In The Mirror? Changing Body Shape And Size

There are more physical changes on the horizon. Maybe you have already noticed that you are growing quickly. During this rapid growth spurt, some boys find that clothes that fit at the beginning of the school year are too small by Halloween! Soon your shoulders will start to get wider and your muscles will start to develop more. You are on your way to achieving your adult body.

One kind of annoying (and possibly embarrassing) part of the rapid increase in size and height is that your arms, legs, hands, and feet may grow faster than the rest of your body. So while the rest of your body is catching up, you might feel a little clumsy. Sooner or later your body will catch up to your arms and legs and you'll be back to your smooth self again.

Eat Right And Shape Up

You probably don't want to hear this but eating right—and we don't mean potato chips for breakfast, cookies for lunch, and candy for dinner—is really important at this time in your life. Your body is working hard to grow larger and stronger and it really needs healthy food to do what it needs to do. Try and eat three healthy meals a day, starting with a nutritious breakfast. Eating fruits and vegetables as much as possible will also help keep you at a healthy weight and give you the energy you need to do all the things you want to do.

And no, french fries do NOT count as a vegetable.

As for exercise, just get outside and do what interests you. If you like bugs, go on a bug hunt. If you like bikes, go for a ride. Don't try and force yourself to do some exercise just to get moving. You won't stick with it. Thirty minutes of moving around, whether that's walking, dancing, skateboarding, gardening, acting, or building a tree house, is all you need to stay healthy and fit.

And no, video games do NOT count as exercise.

Body Hair

A big part of puberty is growing hair in all sorts of places you never had hair before!

Often the first place a boy notices hair growing is above his penis. Usually, the next place he becomes a little furry is the underarms, followed by the face, usually on the upper lip. When this happens, the exciting process of learning to shave is right around the corner. You can read more about shaving in chapter one.

Finally, body hair begins to spread over the legs and arms. This can continue even a few years after all the other big changes of puberty have already happened. Some boys develop chest hair long after puberty, even into their 20s. But not all adult men have chest hair.

Hey, Am I Getting... Breasts?

Actually, boys do have breast tissue under their nipples. About half of all boys develop some swelling under their nipples as a part of middle puberty. The medical name for this is *gynecomastia* and it is a normal reaction to hormonal changes in the body. There are no medications that can make this swelling disappear, it just goes away on its own, usually in about six months. If you feel particularly worried about it, talk to your parents or a health care provider. You might feel it is less noticeable if you wear a shirt that fits loosely in the chest.

When you are between 12 and 14 years old, your voice will start to get deeper. The deepening of your voice happens because of (bet you guessed this by now) the effect of testosterone. This time the testosterone is working on your larynx (also known as your voice box). The larynx then gets bigger and your vocal cords get longer and thicker.

For some boys, the voice change happens almost all at once; it seems like they go to bed one night with the voice of a boy and wake up the next morning with the voice of a man. Other guys may have months where their voice is higher at one moment and then lower a moment later.

KNOW THE FACTS

A boy's vocal chords grow 60% longer during puberty and become thicker. They go from vibrating 200 times a second to 120 times a second.

Sometimes a very quick change in pitch comes out as cracking. This might happen at very inconvenient moments: when you ask a question in class or when you are just about to get to the punch line of a joke. Fortunately, voice changes seldom take longer than 3-4 months to work themselves out.

What's That Smell?
Changes In Your Skin

You may have noticed (or someone might have told you!) that you are starting to smell, and not like a flower! As you go through puberty, the sweat and sebaceous (oil) glands in your skin become more active. This makes you sweat more. Because of hormonal changes, your sweat also has a different (some people say stronger) smell.

Your sebaceous glands are also pumping out more oil and this is part of what causes acne (also called "pimples" or the slang name "zits") in boys going through puberty. Acne and smelliness are normal, but there are ways you can take care of your skin to help decrease problems with both. You can read more about this in chapter one.

The Expert Says

Sweating is a healthy part of being active, so don't be embarrassed if you smell a bit after an intense game of basketball. Just take a shower as soon as you can.

Quick Tip

Keeping a journal can help you feel more in control of your emotions. Getting those feelings out of your head and down on paper might help you understand a bit better why you are feeling like you do. You don't have to let anyone read (or even know about) the journal. It can be your secret. You can keep a journal on your computer (called a blog) or get a special notebook put your thoughts in.

Emotional Changes

Have you ever gotten to the point where you are happy one moment, furious the next, and then sad half an hour later? Welcome to one of the hardest parts of puberty: mood swings.

There are at least two reasons for mood swings. The first is the hormonal changes that are going on in your body. Yes, that pesky testosterone strikes again! The second has to do with your changing place in the world. Puberty is the bridge between being a boy and being a man, and sometimes you might feel like you don't belong either place. You aren't a kid anymore, but sometimes you feel like one inside and still want to do kid things. On the other hand, you aren't ready for the responsibilities of an adult, even though you may feel like you want and need more independence. Some days you might feel out of place and

The Expert Says

Everyone is concerned about what other people think of them, how their bodies look, and how they compare to others.

like no one understands what you're going through. No wonder you might be a little (or a lot) cranky sometimes!

Talking about your feelings might help keep those emotions in check. Don't worry if it is hard for you to open up. Everyone feels this way sometimes. A trusted adult will understand if it is difficult for you to get the words out.

Reviewing: What's Normal

● **First of all, it's normal to feel unsure about the changes in your body.** That's why this book was written, to help you sort out some of the questions you might have.

● **It's also normal to develop more slowly or quickly than your friends and other boys you know.** Every boy has his own pace for physical and emotional development.

● **It's normal to feel unsettled about yourself and your relationships.** Puberty is a very confusing and sometimes awkward time… for everyone. Right now feeling weird is perfectly normal!

● **It's normal to have embarrassing things—like your voice cracking during a presentation—happen to you.** At the time, it may seem like the worst thing that's ever happened in your life, but in a few weeks or a few months you'll forget all about it.

● **It's normal to want to make changes in your life.** You're growing up and things aren't supposed to stay the same.

● **So don't sweat it.** It may take a little while, but sooner or later, you'll find that all these changes have sorted themselves out and you feel…perfectly normal!

CHAPTER 3

Your Changing Body In The Outside World

SCHOOL: Grades

As you get older, parents and teachers (and therefore, kids) talk a lot more about grades. Some schools give marks like "satisfactory" or "needs improvement" in earlier years, but by third grade, many schools have switched to the more common A, B, C (well, you know the rest...) system. This makes a lot of kids nervous because they seem more like "real" grades, something that will count and cause them trouble in the future if they don't do well.

Sometimes boys put lots of pressure on other boys to NOT do well in school because they don't think it's "cool" to get good grades. If this is happening to you, talk with an adult you trust about it. This can be a hard situation to handle, especially if the kids who are teasing you about your good grades are old friends. You've probably heard the term **"peer pressure"** (pressure other kids put on you to be, act, or dress like them) and this is a perfect example. See chapter five for tips on dealing with peer pressure. One thing an adult can do is help you figure out ways to meet other kids who like to study and don't mind being thought of as "smart." Also, ask your teacher for help in keeping your grades private. Teachers sometimes like to praise their best students in front of the other kids, but he or she might not know about the trouble it is causing you!

True or false. If you get a good grade it means you've learned a lot. If you get a bad grade, you haven't learned anything.

Answer: False!

Grades are one way of showing how much you've learned, but they aren't perfect. Sometimes a lower grade in a hard subject means you actually learned more than a higher grade in subject that's easy for you.

True or false. Even smart kids can sometimes get bad grades or have a hard time in school.

Answer: True!

The grades that you see on your report card do NOT mean "dumb" or "smart." There are lots of kinds of intelligence. Even if school is not that easy for you, you can bet that you have special skills somewhere else, even if you haven't discovered them yet.

True or false. If you are getting a bad grade in a subject, just give up, quit school, and move to Australia, there's nothing you can do to change it.

Answer: False!

Just because you are getting low grades in a subject, it doesn't mean you aren't good at that subject, or that your grade in that subject has to stay low. Talk to your teacher about what you need to do to bring the grade up.

True or false. You should like all subjects equally. If you don't like math and spelling the same amount, there is something very, very wrong with you.

Answer: False!

It's normal to have some subjects that you like and some subjects that you don't. After all, haven't grown-ups been asking you "What's your favorite subject?" since kindergarten. In fact, if you do the homework for the classes you like least first, you can use the homework for the classes you like more as a reward for yourself!

If you are having trouble in school, you can get help from:

a. Your teacher after school

b. Summer camp

c. After-school study groups

d. Your neighborhood library

e. An adult at home

f. The guy who feeds the lions at the zoo

Yes, you guessed it, every one but "F." And you could ask the guy at the zoo, but please don't distract him while he's feeding the lion. If he ends up being cat food he won't be able to be much help to you.

This is the time to start keeping a little notebook (or a big, huge notebook if you need it) where you write down all your assignments and check them off when they're done. You'll be able to have more fun hanging out after school if you can look at your notebook and see you've got everything taken care of! You can also use your assignment notebook to remind you of the things you need to take to school in the morning.

Study Skills

There isn't room in this book for all the information we could include about study skills. If you are interested in learning more about how to study, your school librarian can point you to entire books on the subject. However, there are a few simple things you can do right now to make your study time more effective:

● Set aside a special time to study every day. For some kids, right after they get home from school works. Other kids need a break and prefer to dig into their books after they get something to eat and have some time to relax or do other chores.

● Find a quiet place to study. If home doesn't work, try your school or community library.

● Don't wait until the night before a project is due to start it. If you have any questions or don't understand something you won't have time to get the answers you need.

Getting Along With Teachers

If you ever want to get a grown-up talking, ask them to tell you about their favorite teacher. Then ask them about their least favorite teacher. Never ask these questions if you have somewhere to be soon; those questions usually lead to very long stories!

The fact that grown-ups will talk so fondly about things that happened so long ago might remind you how important teachers are to ALL kids. Hopefully, you've already had

Learning begins when you say, "I don't know."

a few teachers that you really liked. Probably you've had some teachers that you didn't like as much. This is very normal.

Although you might not have a lot (or any) choice about who your teachers are right now, you do have choices about what to do when you have a difficult teacher/student situation.

If a teacher is getting on your nerves, it might be tempting to think, "you're not the boss of me." Except for well, when you are at school, they are the boss of you. If you are having trouble getting along with a teacher, try and think of it as a chance to learn a very important grown-up skill. Just like a boy might have to learn from a teacher he might not like, grown-ups sometimes have to work for bosses they don't get along with. It might not be easy for you, but there are some things you can try to help your school-life go more smoothly.

One thing you can do if you are having trouble getting along with a teacher is to try and give it a little time. Especially at the beginning of the year, teachers have a lot to do with setting up their classrooms and getting books and supplies ready. You might find

I don't think much of a man who is not wiser today than he was yesterday.

—ABRAHAM LINCOLN

Quick Tip

Even if it seems like a teacher is being unfair or harsh with you, make sure you are "taking care of business." If you know you are doing everything you are supposed to be doing in the classroom, you can feel proud of yourself and the teacher will know you are doing everything you can to do well in the class. For example, are you coming to class on time and with everything you need? Are you turning in assignments when they are due? Are you following the special rules the teacher has established in his or her classroom? Are you asking questions when you don't understand? Finally, are you doing your best? Sometimes teachers are hardest on good students who they know can be great students.

they act differently when things settle down, further into the school year. Since every boy and every teacher is different, it might take you and the teacher time to figure each other out.

If things don't seem to be getting better, talk to an adult you trust. This can be a parent, family friend, etc. You are probably already talking to someone your own age. This is good for letting off steam, but other kids might not have the experience to help you completely sort out the problem.

If none of this helps, ask an adult if they would help you set up a meeting with the teacher. Sometimes just talking about the problem directly, especially if you have an adult who understands you and can help you explain yourself if you get stuck, can really help a lot.

As you go through school, you will have some teachers who you feel really close to and some that you can't wait to say goodbye to at the end of the year. If you can figure out how to learn from all different types of teachers, you will have some very important life skills that will help you a lot in later years.

Reach out to the teachers you admire.

Let's Play: Boys And Sports

Boys often feel pressure to be good at sports. This pressure may come from family members, parents, coaches, or friends. Sometimes this pressure comes from a desire to be popular or to be a part of a particular group. Many boys enjoy identifying themselves as athletes. Some even dream of making it to the big leagues.

The Expert Says

Good sportsmanship—learning how to be both a good winner and a good loser—is an important part of playing sports.

Playing a sport well is great, but the goal should be to enjoy yourself. Only a few young men will grow up to be professional athletes, but every boy can be part of a team. Here are just a few reasons to get involved in the sport of your choice. You could:

- Have fun
- Get exercise, enjoy what your body can do
- Learn skills (like how to dribble and how to pass but also things like discipline and teamwork)
- Make friends
- Relieve stress and pent up energy

Please notice "win every game" is not listed as a reason. It is fun to win. But if there

Sports Safety

Sports accidents do happen, but there are lots of things you can do to prevent them.

One of the most important things you can do is to wear your protective gear. Your head is super-important and one of the easiest parts of your body to protect; simply wear the helmet made for the sport you're playing. Have your coach adjust the helmet for you and always use the chin strap if the helmet comes with one. Otherwise, your helmet might go flying one way and you flying the other at the exact moment when you should be sticking together!

For some sports, like soccer and football, you might also need protective pads. Wear them, even if they are uncomfortable, or you might be much more uncomfortable later!

Also very important: protecting your genital area. Two pieces of equipment can help you protect your penis and testicles. These things are an athletic supporter (also known as a "jockstrap" or a "jock") and a cup. A cup is a hard piece of triangular plastic that, despite its name, looks nothing like a drinking cup. It goes inside your jockstrap and protects your genitals from direct blows, either from another player (for example, during a tackle or a tag play at home) or from equipment (the ball, a flying bat, etc). When you are in a hurry it might feel like wearing a cup and jock

are too much bother. But if you've ever been hit by a ground ball that takes a bad hop, you know that even with a cup, it can be very painful. Without a cup you risk permanent damage. If other boys in the locker room give you a hard time about wearing a jock or a cup, tell them to mind their own business, or do the final necessary adjustments in the bathroom stall so the protection of your private parts is kept private.

Another very important way you can keep from being injured when you play sports is to warm up and stretch out before you start. Warming up and stretching give your muscles a chance to "wake up." There are special areas of your body you'll need to concentrate on stretching for different sports. Your coach should know all about this. If you are playing a sport (like skateboarding) that doesn't require teams or coaches,

Quick Tip

Wear a pair of baggy boxers over your protective equipment and no one will know you are wearing it.

you can do your own research about stretching out. Someone more experienced in the sport may have some ideas, or you can check your local school or public library for books on the subject.

The final word of advice for staying safe when playing sports: don't play if you are hurt. It's easy to get caught up in the excitement of the final play or a close game. But playing when you are hurt can turn a small, not so serious injury, into one that can give you problems for a long time. Anyone who asks

you to play when you are actually injured is not respecting your body.

The Expert Says

Sometimes parents behave worse than the kids when it comes to sports. Try not to let it get to you if the adults around you are taking the game too seriously.

is too much emphasis on winning, sports become less fun. Think about it: if the only thing that makes sports fun is winning, and only one team can win, that means only half the players get to enjoy it! Would you and a bunch of your friends get together and go to a movie that you knew half of you would hate? No, it would be a waste of time and money. Sports are the same way if the only goal is winning.

If losing is particularly hard for you, you can set personal goals for each game that don't depend on winning or losing. For example, if you are an outfielder, your goal could be to catch 80 percent of the fly balls that come to you. If you are struggling to be supportive of your teammates, you could have the goal of finding five things to compliment your fellow players about.

Sometimes adults will push boys too hard. While pushing yourself a little can be good, pushing yourself and your growing body too hard can lead to permanent injuries. If you are feeling so much pressure that sports have lost some of their fun for you, it might be time to talk to the adults in your life about this.

You win some, you lose some, but you always try again.

Other Extracurricular Activities

Sometimes boys think that if they aren't good at sports, they can't be a part of things. But that's just not true. Even if you don't like the sports teams at school, there are many other activities you can get involved in. Plus, school is not the only place to be on teams! Sometimes you can find different kinds of teams or learn how to play different sports at your community recreational center or through camps or clubs. And most schools, especially as you get older, have many different kinds of opportunities for having fun and making friends and learning what you are good at.

If your school doesn't offer an activity you'd like, maybe you can suggest it. If you can't find any groups or clubs you like at your school, often community centers, youth centers, and religious organizations have activities for boys as well.

Non-Sports Activities

Don't like sports? No problem! Try:

- Writing for the school paper
- Taking pictures for the yearbook
- Playing chess on the school chess team or in the school chess club
- Singing in the choir
- Acting in (or making sets or designing costumes for) the school play
- Running for student government
- Helping plan dances or other fun events (many schools have a social committee for things like this)
- Learning about running and fixing electronic equipment in the AV club
- Learning about culture and language in (for example) a Spanish club
- Performing a stand up comedy routine in the school talent show
- Playing a musical instrument
- Volunteering as a tutor to someone who needs help
- Working behind the scenes for a sports team keeping score or helping the coach

The best way to predict your future is to create it.

Going To College

You might already be thinking about college, or you might not yet. It's still early so try and keep your mind open to all the possibilities. Even if no one in your family has been to college, or your family doesn't have a lot of money, it is still possible for you to get a higher education. There are a lot of options such as scholarships and other types of financial aid. You can also spend your first two years at a community college which is usually much less expensive than going to a private four-year school.

While college isn't for everyone, going to college can open your eyes to some of the less obvious careers out there. Plus, a good education can help you not only get a job that pays more money, but also to have many more jobs to choose from.

However, a college degree is not the only way to get a job

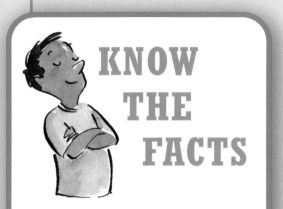

KNOW THE FACTS

A college graduate can be expected to earn more than a million dollars more over the course of his life than someone with just a high school diploma.

Getting An After School Job

Getting a job after school is a great way to expand your horizons and make some money at the same time. While you may be too young yet to hold a job in a store or restaurant (two of the more common after-school jobs for teenagers) there are plenty of jobs out there for someone your age. For example, you could mow lawns or shovel snow. You could babysit for your neighbors. You could walk dogs or water plants for people who are on vacation.

Two of the most important things you will learn from having an after-school job are to take responsibility for the work you do and to do your work the best you can. You'll also learn how

you enjoy. There are some jobs that require specialized training, but not college. Some jobs (such as being a plumber) require you to complete an apprenticeship. An apprenticeship is where you spend time learning from an experienced person in that profession, but not in a formal classroom setting.

hard you have to work to make money, which will help you appreciate all that your parents have given you. Finally, you'll have money to go to the movies and do the other things you like to do.

Considering Your Future

One of the benefits in getting involved in fun activities outside of regular schoolwork is that you can learn more about what you're good at and what you like to do. These things might have nothing to with your regularly scheduled classes. You can also meet more adults and get some ideas about jobs you might like to consider for a future career.

Besides extracurricular activities, there are lots of other ways to find out about different jobs. If you think you might be interested in, for example, growing tulips for a living, but you live in Arizona and don't know anyone who grows anything but a cactus now and then, try finding a book about the subject. Or ask an adult or teacher to help you find some information on-line. Also, some colleges include career information for younger students on their websites.

Even if you don't have any career ideas floating around in your head at this point, don't worry. While it's helpful to be thinking about what talents you have and what you can be involved in that will nurture those talents, doing well in school and participating in extracurricular activities is a good start.

It's great to have a really certain idea about what you would like to do for work when you get older, but it's also okay to change your mind a lot! There are lots of adults who still aren't sure what they want to be when they grow up!

Quick Tip

Instead of spending your money on candy and other small stuff, save the money you earn from your job to buy something big you really want. If you save up enough, you'll be the envy of your friends when you buy your first car.

CHAPTER 4

Changes
At Home

All Sorts Of Families

You might have noticed this book mostly talks about the "adults in your life" or "adults at home" instead of using the more specific "parents." That's because not all boys are raised by their parents. Some boys are raised by a single parent, grandparents, two moms, two dads, in foster families, blended families, by aunts and uncles, and combinations of the above. We want those boys to understand that this book is for them, too. Every family is unique and different from every other family. What's important is that you have an adult in your life who you can trust.

What Do These People Want From Me?

The process of going from being a kid to being an adult is mostly about taking more and more responsibility for more and more bits of your life. This goes on until you are managing most of your everyday choices yourself, or until you become, as the saying goes, "the boss of you." The truth is you're never totally the boss of you. We live in a complex society. Even when you are an adult there will be some people (your boss at work, the police, your girlfriend) who will have the power to enforce consequences if you don't follow the rules. Of course, your boss probably won't give you a bedtime or tell you what kind of TV shows you can watch!

Most of the common everyday conflicts that happen between boys in the transition between childhood and adulthood and their parents centers around issues of responsibility. A parent thinks a boy isn't responsible enough, for example, to make choices about seeing a certain movie or going to a certain party. The boy thinks he definitely is. Sound familiar? Of course, the opposite can be true as well. A parent thinks a boy is old enough to mow the lawn

and take out the trash, the boy thinks that's too much responsibility for someone his age.

Some conflict between teens and pre-teens and the adults in their lives is normal, even healthy. You've probably noticed you don't have control over what your parents do. But you do have control over what you do. One big step you can take towards getting to do more things you want to do is to work on building your parents' trust in you. The easiest way to do this is to do WHAT you say you are going to do WHEN you say you're going to do it. If you agree to help your little brother with his homework after school, take the time to help, even if you'd really rather watch something (anything even) on TV. If your parents

Quick Tip

Offer to call or text message your parents to check in when you are out with friends. Always have a plan for getting out of unsafe situations.

give you a time to be home, make sure you're there on time, even if everyone else has a later curfew and is bugging you to stay just a "few more minutes." If you say you are going to a party, be at that party, not somewhere else, unless you call and get permission first.

The Care And Feeding Of Parents: How To Talk So They'll Listen

What else can you do to help your relationship with your parents go better? Lots of things. For example:

● If you end up in a mess, confess early and ask for help. You are going to make mistakes sometimes. Most parents remember this. Covering up a mess almost always guarantees a bigger disaster in the end.

● Tell them how you're feeling. It may seem like they can read your mind, but they can't.

● Treat your parents like people. They are! Try talking about something they are interested in. (Hint: it's probably not video games.)

● Try not to roll your eyes at them. Eye-rolling often drives even the calmest parents wild.

● If you are in the middle of a discussion that is turning into an argument, ask to take a break and calm down.

● Listen to your parents. Ask questions. Show that you are trying, at least, to understand their point of view.

Curfews And Other Rules

Curfews are often a hot button issue for adults and kids. This is a perfect time for you to work on the art of the compromise. Sometimes parents will let you come in later if they know you are safe when you are out. Work with them on what you would do if, for example, you got to a party and there wasn't an adult there, or kids were drinking. If they know you have a way to stay safe, they'll feel better about being flexible with your curfew.

KNOW THE FACTS

The average curfew for a 13-year-old boy is 9pm weeknights and 10pm on weekends.

If you and your parents are constantly fighting about rules in the house, ask for more details about their expectations. For example, a common rule adults make is "kids must keep their rooms clean." Well, to you, "clean" might mean "no fungus growing on the carpet." To your parents, "clean" might mean that your bed is made every day and that you vacuum twice a week.

Special Family Situations: Stressed Families

Every family has stress, but some families have much more stress to deal with than others. For example, some families have to cope with having very little money, someone in the family drinking too much or using drugs, homelessness, or living in a neighborhood with a lot of crime. Sometimes (not always) situations like this make it hard for the adults in the family to be consistent with discipline and providing for kids' needs, even if they are trying very hard. Sometimes these adults need help so that they can be the kind of parents they want to be.

If you are afraid of someone in your family, or aren't getting your basic needs (clothing, food, going to the doctor) met, or your family is super-stressed in some way, it's very important that you talk to someone. Your school guidance counselor or school nurse can be good people to start with. It might be really hard to ask for help, but it is very brave. Kids from stressed out families do NOT have to be messed up.

Divorce

Although it isn't always as dramatic as some of the situations just mentioned, divorce can also be very hard on kids. The most important thing to remember if your parents are getting divorced is: it is never, ever, ever (are you listening?) the kids' fault. Divorce is a choice adults make for adult reasons. Even if you were super extra good and never teased your little sister again, or if you were super extra bad and made her life completely miserable, you couldn't cause (or prevent) your parents' divorce.

When parents break up, there is often a lot of shuffling around of kids, and you may have to adjust to having two homes instead of one, or even (later) having a new step-parent or step-siblings. This can be really difficult, especially at first. If you are having trouble with this, it's important to talk with your parents directly, rather than acting out your feelings with bad behavior. With bad behavior you might get you the attention you need, but it will be negative, not positive attention.

The Expert Says

Divorce is one of the most stressful things a kid can deal with, but there are ways to make the situation as easy as it can be. Here are a few tips:

● Divorce is more difficult for a family if the parents can't get along at all. Ask your parents to do their best to keep the peace when you are around.

● Be fair to both of your parents. Try not to take sides. If your parents have a disagreement, try to stay out of it.

● Accept that some changes will happen. You may have to change schools or even move. You'll get used to your life sooner if you try to look at the positive aspects of it.

● Some families have money problems as parents try to adjust to having two homes and two lives instead of one. You may have to change your spending habits and your expectations of gifts at special occassions.

● Talk to someone. Don't keep your feelings inside. There are people out there who care about you and want to help.

Oh Brother (And Oh Sister): The Art Of Being Friends With Siblings

Brothers and sisters can be really fun, but that doesn't mean it's easy for siblings to get along. Some things that might help:

It is common for younger kids to feel like their older siblings get to "have all the fun" and do whatever they want. Older brothers and sisters often think that the baby of the family gets more than his or her share of attention. Try and remember that there are good things and bad things about whenever you came into your family, and most times these things are pretty even in the end.

Don't be confused if you feel both proud AND jealous of your siblings, sometimes even at the exact same time. If you are feeling jealous of what your siblings have done, remind yourself that you have special skills and talents that they don't have.

Did you know you can make "just between siblings" rules? For example, if you and your brother have run into problems when you tease each other, you could agree never to tease each other where other (non-family members) can hear. Or you can agree never to tease each other about certain things.

Older brothers and sisters can really help make this time in your life easier if you ask them. If you're the oldest, remember to be there for your younger siblings when they get to be your age.

Quick Tip

If you are sharing a room with a sibling, keep one small section (even if it is part of a closet or the top of your desk) as yours. Having a private spot to keep private things can help you feel safe.

You might not believe it now, but your brothers and sisters may be the best friends you have throughout your life. If you invest in your relationship with them now, it will really pay off later on.

CHAPTER 5

Your Changing Feelings And Friends

Your Friends

As if it isn't enough that your body and your feelings are changing, many boys find this is an age where they have to make a whole new group of friends!

Sometimes this happens because you are going to a bigger middle school and the kids you used to hang out with are in different classes and have a different schedule than you. Sometimes the crowd that you hung out with when you were younger starts doing things you don't like and you need to find a new crowd to hang out with. Sometimes you just find that your interests have changed and you don't have anything in common with your old friends anymore. Whatever the reason, making new friends can be scary but ultimately rewarding.

A Few Tips For Making New Friends:

Some friendships just happen, but more often you need to make a special effort to find good friends. Here are a few ways to start.

Being friendly (waving to people, smiling, cracking jokes with them) is a good beginning. Be interested in your new potential friend. Ask him questions about his likes and dislikes, how things are going for him, or what kinds of things he likes to do after school.

One way of really cementing a friendship is by doing things together besides watching TV and playing video games. Activities that don't require you to interact much can't help you get to know your friend very well. Try going to the park, going on an adventure, or building something together instead.

If you want to change crowds, you can sometimes start by making a few new friends. Eat lunch with someone new, chat with him between classes. You can find things you have in common this way.

The Expert Says

Trust is one of the most important traits a new friend can offer. If you can't trust someone, he can't be a good friend to you.

If you are having trouble finding and keeping good friends, you might try making a list of the qualities (for example, sense of humor, likes to do the same things, even-tempered) that you are looking for in a friend. Look around to see who has those qualities: it might be someone you weren't expecting!

Although it is more common for boys your age to have boys as their close friends, girls can also be great friends. Sometimes other kids—or even grown-ups—want to make a big deal about a girl/boy friendship, acting as if it is something romantic or teasing you about it. If you repeat calmly, "yes, she is a girl and she is my friend" the person teasing you will get bored and move on to another topic of conversation.

This is a time in your life when you are exploring relationships and getting to know yourself better. While you might sometimes have romantic feelings or crushes, don't put pressure on yourself to start that part of your life too soon. If you are interested in dating or "going with" someone, work on being friends first. Try different fun activities where you can really get to know the other person. Going to the movies, which is a very typical first date, doesn't allow much time for talking, so it might not be the best way to get to know someone. In fact, it will be less pressure for both of you if you go out with a few other friends (they can be on a date or not) for a group activity.

Quick Tip

Don't assume that someone doesn't want to be friends just because they don't say hi to you. The person could be really shy and afraid to make the first move.

Friendship Skills

Although in some ways it's natural to be a good friend to someone you care about, there are skills that can make being a good friend easier.

For example, everyone makes mistakes in friendships. We say something that we don't mean when we are tired or angry, or we let our good-natured teasing go too far. One of the surest ways to keep a friendship growing strong is to apologize when you do something to hurt your friend's feelings. It works best if you don't say, "I'm sorry but..." and then go on to explain to the person why they are wrong. That's not really an apology! It's a way of keeping an argument going!

Another thing that helps keep a friendship growing is talking through disagreements before they get really big. If a friend borrows your baseball glove and doesn't bring it back when he promised to, it's better to mention it the first time he does it and not wait until the tenth time and blow up. He might not even know that it bothers you until you tell him.

Being a good listener is one of the most important friendship-building skills you can have. Sometimes it can be hard to listen. Your friend might want to talk about a movie that you thought was stupid. Interrupting with *"booooorrring"* might make your friend laugh the first time, but it won't feel great when he does it back to you. If you make the extra effort to pay attention to what your friend has to say, you might become more interested in the conversation and decide the movie wasn't so stupid after all!

"But Everyone Is Doing It": Dealing With Peer Pressure

The biggest thing to remember about peer pressure is that whatever "it" is, everyone is **not** doing it. Resisting peer pressure can be hard. Some boys say it is one of the most difficult things about these in-between years. Here are some tricks you can use when dealing with other kids who want you to do something you don't want to do:

Practice saying "no" when it isn't super important. This will help you be thought of as someone who doesn't just go along with the crowd. Often kids will stop pressuring you if they know you aren't going to give in because it makes them look silly.

Physically remove yourself from situations in which you feel pressure to do something you don't want to do. If you know that the boys in the corner at recess are going to be plotting their next wedgie victim and you don't want to be part of the mean wedgie-giving gang, don't walk by them. Take the long way around.

Ask a good friend or a trusted adult to help you brainstorm ways to deal with things kids say when they are trying to get you to do some-thing you don't want to do. Make up flash cards to carry around with you to remind you what to say.

Have a "peer pressure" buddy. If your friend sees you struggling to say "no" to something everyone else seems to be saying "yes" to, he can jump in with, "Well, I'm not going to do it either." Having one person on your side feels totally different than going it alone. Make sure you return the favor for your friend!

The biggest thing that can help you deal with peer pressure is feeling confident in yourself and in your abilities. As you get involved and find things you are good at, you will feel stronger to resist the pressure because you know more about who you are and what you want in life.

"Ouch": Staying Safe
In Relationships
With Other People

Peer pressure is different than bullying. If some-one says you won't be cool if you don't do something, that's peer pressure. If someone says they are going to beat you up if you don't do something, that's bullying. If this happens, let a trusted adult know right away. They can help you find ways to stay safe.

Bullying is not the only way that kids can get hurt, which is why it's important to know about the boundaries between you and other people.

You probably already know the message that your body is yours and that no one (except for sometimes a doctor in a doctor's office) has the right to touch you in your private areas (the area covered by your bathing suit).

Another place it's important to follow safety guidelines is on the internet. Your parents have certainly warned you about not talking with strangers. Remember that almost everyone on the internet is a stranger! Make sure you tell a parent or another adult if someone you don't know (even if they say they are a kid) contacts you in a chat room or through e-mail.

Check out www.isafe.org for more internet safety tips.

"I Am Driving Even Myself Crazy!" Dealing With Out Of Control Feelings

Earlier in this book we talked about the extra hormones in your body and how they might make you feel moody. You may feel cranky and ready to run away from home one minute, and want to hug everyone and do a little happy dance the next. No matter how much your teachers, your parents, and even this book reminds you "this is normal," it's still no fun.

There are things you can do with this extra emotional energy though. Some things that many boys find works for them:

● Try not to get too over-tired or too hungry. Hunger and tiredness can cause crankiness all by themselves, and adding them to your hormonal mix makes things much worse!

● Remember that feelings are not good or bad, they just are. Yes, it's more fun to feel happy than to feel sad. But it isn't wrong to feel sad. In fact, feelings give you information about yourself and your world. For example, if you always feel irritated or angry after you spend time with a certain friend, maybe there is something happening that you need to talk with that friend about.

● Writing in a journal can help you deal with strong emotions. Writing about what is going on with your feelings not only can help release some of the extra emotional energy but also can help you figure things out.

● Sometimes physical activity helps get out all your stored up emotional energy when nothing else can. That might even be why schools started having recess! You can shoot hoops, or ride your bike, or even just go for a long walk. If you're at home and can't get away and do anything else, sometimes just yelling into a pillow will work wonders!

● Talking can help, too. If you just want to let off steam, your best friend might be able to help you. If you need some guidance or advice, a trusted adult who respects your boundaries is also a good choice.

● If nothing else works, get involved in a fun activity that will get your mind off of your strong feelings. You can play a musical instrument, listen to your favorite CD, read, or complete an art project. Overall, try not to dwell on your feelings. Chances are in an hour you'll feel differently.

Is It Okay To Cry?

This is a question a lot of boys ask because this is the age when people start telling them, "you're getting to be a man now, you have to stop all the tears."

You don't have to stop all the tears. In fact, it's really important to cry when you need to. Crying is a release of strong feelings, and if you don't ever have that release, it can cause you problems in your mental and physical health.

It's unfortunate that there are some people who will make you feel worse if you cry in front of them, or make it harder for you by teasing you. If you are around a lot of people like that, it can help to make a deal with a really good friend. Agree that part of your friendship is being each other's "safe-space" and that you will never tease each other about crying.

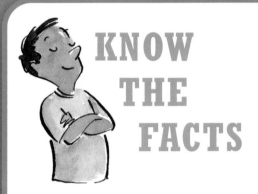

KNOW THE FACTS

The tears you cry because you are sad have different chemicals in them than tears that form when your eyes water. Crying actually releases chemicals that your body is trying to get rid of. So think of crying as "taking out the trash" so your body feels better. Don't keep the trash around. Cry if you need to.

Self Esteem

You are just getting to know yourself in these years and you are going to find out you have many amazing qualities. You are different than everyone else on the planet and your uniqueness is what makes you on the way to becoming a "real man." Some men like to watch sports and some men like to play sports. Some men HATE sports and would rather work on their woodworking projects during their time off. Some men think flowers are stinky and some men love to spend time arranging them. Some men spend their weekends doing extreme sports, and some men think extreme sports are extremely stupid. None of these men are wrong.

Respect the way you are inside and say good things to yourself. Try to find and be around people who appreciate you and what you have to give. You are growing now, and you have more growing to do, but you are on your way to becoming a man, a strong and caring force in the world.

Websites

Name of website: Preteen Health Talk

Where is it? http://www.pamf.org/preteen/

Who runs it? The Palo Alto Medical Foundation

Lots of information about your changing body can be found here. Also includes sections on your feelings, growing up, and sharing. Another unique feature of this site is that it includes books and movies reviewed by both kids and parents!

Name of website: Are You a Working Teen?

Where is it? http://www.cdc.gov/niosh/adoldoc.html

Who runs it? National Institute for Occupational Safety and Health

Useful information about health and safety in the workplace; a perfect introduction as you as you prepare for your first job.

Name of website: BAM! Body And Mind

Where is it? http://www.bam.gov/

Who runs it? Department of Health and Human Services

This is a huge site that includes information about diseases, food and nutrition, stress, family matters and conflict resolution (getting along). Also includes games and quizzes and really fun interactive stuff like a create your own activity calendar, an interactive game that tests your bully smarts, and a stress-o-meter quiz.

Name of website: Infection Detection Protection

Where is it? http://www.amnh.org/nationalcenter/infection/

Who runs it? The American Museum of Natural History in New York

This site is about your immune system and germs. You can play some interesting games like "Meet the Microbes," "How Lou Got the Flu," and "Bacteria in the Cafeteria" here.

Name of website: What do You Like?

Where is it? http://www.bls.gov/k12/

Who runs it? Bureau of Labor Statistics

You can find career information about many different types of jobs here, written especially for kids.

Name of website: Environmental Kids

Where is it? http://www.epa.gov/kids/

Who runs it? The Environmental Protection Agency

This site is about things you can do to make your environment safer for you and your family. It includes information on recycling, water use, and solid waste. Includes helpful fact based information (like for school reports) as well as explanations of projects you can get involved in yourself.

Name of website: Healthfinder for Kids

Where is it? http://www.healthfinder.gov/kids/

Who runs it? U.S. Department of Health and Human Services

This is a very easy to use website where you can find information about everything from exercise to nutrition to safety and alcohol and drugs. Also includes a page that links to more than 90 places on the web where you can learn about health by playing on-line games.

Name of website: TeensHealth

Where is it? http://www.kidshealth.org/teen/your_mind/families/divorce.html

Who runs it? The Nemours Foundation's Center for Children's Health Media

A good place to find lots of information on dealing with divorce and other teen issues. Also available in Spanish.

Name of website: Get it Straight: The Facts About Drugs

Where is it? http://www.dea.gov/pubs/straight/cover.htm

Who runs it? U.S. Department of Justice Drug Enforcement Administration

From smoking to drinking to steroids, this website covers it all including a "teens ask teens" section where you can correspond with other kids and ask any question you might have.

Books

Feed Your Head: Some Excellent Stuff on Being Yourself

By Earl Hipp

(Hazelden, 1991)

This is an older book, but it has a ton of helpful information about resisting peer pressure.

Our Boys Speak

by John Nikkah

(St Martins, 2000)

This book is made up of letters and essays written by young boys. It is broken up into sections by topics like sibling, peer pressure, depression and school violence. You might find it interesting how many other boys are having feelings and struggles just like yours!

Meet Our Experts

James Bierma is a guidance counselor for the St. Paul, MN school district, where he also counsels, mentors, and tutors students in homeless shelters. Mr. Bierma is also the President of the American School Counselor Association and is a co-writer of the school counseling standards for the National Board of Professional Teaching Standards.

Dr. William Fullard is a Professor of Educational Psychology at Temple University. He received his Ph.D. from the University of Pennsylvania. His interests include adolescent cognitive and personality development. He has published research on adolescent sexuality, adolescent parenting practices, and adolescent temperament.

Michael Stevenson was named the Coach of the Year by the National Youth Sports Coaches Association in 2005. He helped write the physical education curriculum for the Clark County, Nevada, School District, where he is also a teacher. He has coached at least three separate sports teams a year since 2000.

Meet the Author and Illustrator

Kelli Dunham is a nurse, stand-up comic, and author of two books, *How to Survive and Maybe Even Love Nursing School* and *How to Survive and Maybe Even Love Your Life as a Nurse.* She has worked as a primary care and home visiting nurse with first-time new moms. She has lived in Port-au-Prince, Haiti, Ohio, Oklahoma, Florida, Portland, Oregon, New York, and on a houseboat in Philadelphia. In her spare time she likes to read and skateboard, and she would really, really like to learn to play the banjo.

Steve Bjorkman has illustrated more than 70 books for children, including picture books such as *Good Night, Little One,* easy readers such as *Thanksgiving Is...,* and series such as *Mama Rex and T.* Steve is also well known for illustrating greeting cards. More than 100 million of his greeting cards for Recycled Paper Greetings have been sold.

Index

About Applesauce Press

What kid doesn't love Applesauce!

Applesauce Press was created to press out the best children's books found anywhere. Like our parent company, Cider Mill Press Book Publishers, we strive to bring fine reading, information, and entertainment to kids of all ages. Between the covers of our creatively crafted books, you'll find beautiful designs, creative formats, and most of all, kid-friendly information on important topics. Our Cider Mill bears fruit twice a year, publishing a new crop of titles each spring and fall.

Where Good Books are
Ready for Press

Visit us on the web at
www.cidermillpress.com
or write to us at
12 Port Farm Road
Kennebunkport, Maine 04046